A

Saint Joseph
Prayer Book

FAMILY PUBLICATIONS · OXFORD

ISBN 978-1-907380-03-7

This book has been made possible by a generous donation from
The Theodore Trust

published by
Family Publications
Denis Riches House
66 Sandford Lane, Kennington
Oxford, OX1 5RP
www.familypublications.co.uk

printed in England
through s|s|media ltd

Table of Contents

From the example of St Joseph we all receive a stro *invitation to carry out with fidelity, simplicity and mode.* *the task that Providence has entrusted to us.*

Pope Benedict XVI, 19 March 2(

Think of Joseph

୫୦ର

Speaking to the crowd and to his disciples, Jesus declared: "You have only one Father" (Mt 23:9). There is but one fatherhood, that of God the Father, the one Creator of the world, "of all that is seen and unseen". Yet man, created in the image of God, has been granted a share in this one paternity of God (cf. Eph 3:15). Saint Joseph is a striking case of this, since he is a father, without fatherhood according to the flesh. He is not the biological father of Jesus, whose Father is God alone, and yet he lives his fatherhood fully and completely. To be a father means above all to be at the service of life and growth. Saint Joseph, in this sense, gave proof of great devotion. For the sake of Christ he experienced persecution, exile and the poverty which this entails. He had to settle far from his native town. His only reward was to be with Christ. His readiness to do all these things illustrates the words of Saint Paul: "It is Christ the Lord whom you serve" (Col 3:24). (...)

Each and every one of us was thought, willed and loved by God. Each and every one of us has a role to play in the plan of God: Father, Son and Holy Spirit. If discouragement overwhelms you, think of the faith of Joseph; if anxiety has its grip on you, think of the hope of Joseph, that descendant of Abraham who hoped against hope; if exasperation or hatred seizes you, think of the love of Joseph, who was the first man to set eyes on the human face of God in the person of the Infant conceived by the Holy Spirit in the womb of the Virgin Mary. Let us praise and thank Christ for having drawn so close to us, and for giving us Joseph as an example and model of love for him.

Pope Benedict XVI, *Yaoundé, 18-19 March 2009*

" *Behold, an angel of the Lord appeared to him in a dream, saying, 'Joseph, son of David, do not fear to take Mary your wife, for that which is conceived in her is of the Holy Spirit.'* "

Mt 1:20-21

A Man of silence
୫୦୯

The silence of St Joseph does not demonstrate an empty interior, but rather the fullness of faith that he carries in his heart, and that guides each of his thoughts and actions. A silence through which Joseph, together with Mary, guard the Word of God, known through sacred Scripture, comparing it continually to the events of the life of Jesus; a silence interwoven with constant prayer, a prayer of blessing of the Lord, of adoration of his holy will and of boundless confidence in his providence. It is not exaggerated to say that Jesus will learn – on a human level – precisely from "father" Joseph this intense interior life, which is the condition of authentic righteousness, the "interior righteousness," which one day he will teach to his disciples (cf. Mt 5:20).

Let's allow ourselves to be "infected" by the silence of St Joseph! It is so lacking in this world which is often too noisy, which is not favourable to recollection and listening to the voice of God. ... Let us cultivate interior recollection so as to receive and keep Jesus in our lives.

Pope Benedict XVI, *18 December 2005*

O Saint Joseph, in the silence of your heart, you welcomed the Word of God, communing in the fullness of your faith with the mysterious heavenly plan unfolding in your life. Guide us on the way of recollection, so that we may treasure silence as a place where we can hear the divine voice. Just as you listened to the angel, may we too find true peace in following God's will.

Amen.

JOSEPH · ACCEPIT · CONIUGEM · SUAM

"When Joseph woke from sleep, he did as the angel of th
Lord commanded him; he took his wife."

Mt 1:2

A humble Man
ജ‌ര

*T*he word "just" evokes his moral rectitude, his sincere attachment to the practice of the law and his attitude of total openness to the will of the heavenly Father. Even in difficult and sometimes tragic moments, the humble carpenter of Nazareth never claimed for himself the right to dispute God's plan. He awaited the call from on High and in silence respected the mystery, letting himself be guided by the Lord. Once he received the mission, he fulfils it with docile responsibility. He listens attentively to the angel, when he is asked to take as his wife the Virgin of Nazareth, in the flight into Egypt and in the return to Israel. In few, but significant strokes, the Evangelists describe him as the caring guardian of Jesus, an attentive and faithful husband, who exercises his family authority in a constant attitude of service. Nothing else is said about him in the Sacred Scriptures, but this silence contains the special style of his mission: a life lived in the greyness of everyday life, but with steadfast faith in Providence.

Pope John Paul II, *19 March 2003*

*S*aint Joseph,
You were chosen by God to serve Jesus and Mary as head of the Holy Family. We ask you to protect our families and to watch over the Church. May we too learn to become faithful servants of Jesus Christ and to trust in God's Providence.

Amen.

" And while they were there, the time came for her to b‹
delivered. And she gave birth to her first-born son an‹
wrapped him in swaddling cloths, and laid him in ‹
manger, because there was no place for them in the inn.

Lk 2:6-

Nativity

I have seen a little picture which represents St Joseph with the Divine Infant, who points towards him, saying: *Ite ad Joseph!* To you I say the same, *Go to Joseph!* Have recourse with special confidence to St Joseph, for his protection is most powerful, now above all that he is the Patron of the Universal Church.

Pope Pius IX

*J*oseph caressed the Son as a Babe; he ministered to Him as God. He rejoiced in Him as in the Good One, and he was awe-struck at Him as the Just One, greatly bewildered:

"Who has given me the Son of the Most High to be a Son to me? I was jealous of Your Mother, and I thought to put her away, and I knew not that in her womb was hidden a mighty treasure, that should suddenly enrich my poor estate. David the king sprang of my race, and wore the crown: and I have come to a very low estate, who instead of a king am a carpenter. Yet a crown has come to me, for in my bosom is the Lord of crowns!"

St Ephrem, *Hymn 4 on the Nativity*

*F*ather, you entrusted our Saviour to the care of Saint Joseph. By the help of his prayers may your Church continue to serve its Lord, Jesus Christ, who lives and reigns with you and the Holy Spirit, one God for ever and ever.

Amen.

Joseph your admirable life
Took place in poverty
But you contemplated the beauty
Of Jesus and Mary.

St Thérèse of Lisieux, PN 14

*O*h, what a saint is the glorious St Joseph! He is not only a Patriarch, but the most distinguished among the Patriarchs. He is not merely a confessor, but far more than a confessor, for in him are included the dignity of the bishop, the generosity of the martyr, the excellence of the other saints. St Joseph will obtain for us, if we repose confidence in him, an increase in every kind of virtue, but particularly in those which he possessed in a pre-eminent degree. These are a perfect purity of body and mind, humility, constancy, fortitude, and perseverance: virtues which will render us victorious over our enemies in this life, and enable us to obtain the grace of enjoying in the life to come those rewards which are prepared for the imitators of St Joseph.

St Francis de Sales, *Entretien XIX*

A Prayer by Cardinal Newman
൭൙൫

O Joseph,
make me so blameless and irreproachable
that I should not care though friends saw into my heart
as perfectly as Jesus and Mary saw into thine.
O gain me the grace of holy simplicity and affectionateness,
so that I may love thee, Mary, and, above all, Jesus,
as thou didst love Jesus and Mary.
O holy Joseph, make me like thee in purity, simplicity,
innocence, and devotion.
Jesus, Mary, Joseph, pray for me.

Amen.

" *And they went with haste,
and found Mary and Joseph,
and the babe lying in the manger.* " Lk 2:16

*Inspired by the Gospel, the Fathers of the Church fro
the earliest centuries stressed that just as St Joseph to
loving care of Mary and gladly dedicated himself
Jesus Christ's upbringing, he likewise watches over a
protects Christ's Mystical Body, that is, the Church,
which the Virgin Mary is the exemplar and model.*

John Paul II, Redemptoris Cus

A sublime dignity

𝕰𝕺𝕽

Oh, how divine was the union between Our Lady and the glorious St Joseph, a union which caused the Supreme Good, the Good of all goods, our Lord Himself, to belong to Joseph even as He belonged to Our Lady not by nature but by grace; which made him a sharer in all the possessions of his dear Spouse, and made him continually increase in perfection by his continual communications with her who possessed all virtues in so exalted a degree that no other creature, however pure and spotless, can attain to them! Nevertheless, St Joseph was the one who made the nearest approach; and as a mirror when set before the rays of the sun reflects them perfectly, and another set before the first so vividly repeats them that it is scarcely possible to see which of the two immediately receives them, even so Our Lady, like a most pure mirror, received the rays of the Sun of Justice, which conveyed into her soul all virtues and perfections; and St Joseph, like a second mirror, reflected them so perfectly, that he appeared to possess them in as sublime a degree as did the glorious Virgin herself.

St Francis de Sales, *Entretien XIX*

O God, who in your unspeakable Providence chose blessed Joseph for your most holy Mother's spouse; grant, we beseech you, that we who revere him as our protector upon earth, may become worthy to have him for our intercessor in heaven. We ask this through Christ our Lord.

Amen.

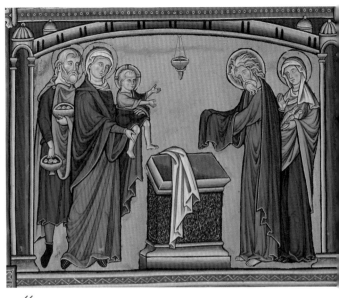

"And when the time came for their purification according to the law of Moses, they brought him up to Jerusalem to present him to the Lord."

Lk 2:21-22

He is that just man,
that wise and loyal servant,
whom you placed at the head of your family.
With a husband's love he cherished Mary,
the virgin Mother of God.
With fatherly care he watched over Jesus Christ your Son,
conceived by the power of the Holy Spirit.

from the Preface of St Joseph

A humble Man raised to a great Destiny

ഇരു

St Joseph is the model of those humble ones that Christianity raises up to great destinies; ... he is the proof that in order to be a good and genuine follower of Christ, there is no need of great things – it is enough to have the common, simple and human virtues, but they need to be true and authentic.

Pope Paul VI, *19 March 1969*

Thanksgiving Prayer for a Child

ഇരു

Saint Joseph, you witnessed the miracle of birth, seeing the infant Jesus born of your most holy spouse, the Virgin Mary. With wonder and awe, you took into your arms the Saviour. With gratitude that only a parent can know, you glorified God for the birth of his Son, entrusted to your fatherly care.

Like you, St Joseph, I too give praise and glory to God for the birth of my child. This child's life is such a miraculous testimony of God's loving presence. My heart is filled with grateful joy. Join me dear St Joseph, in offering thanks to God for the gift of my child.

What great trust and confidence God placed in you, St Joseph, by entrusting his only Son into your fatherly care. This inspires me to entrust the spiritual care and protection of my child into your caring and loving hands. Teach, guide, and support me to fulfil well my vocation to be a worthy parent to this child.

Amen.

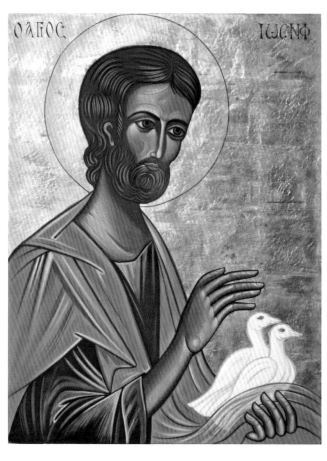

O ΔΓΙΟC   ΙΩCΝΦ

" ... and to offer a sacrifice according to the custom
of the law of the Lord 'a pair of turtledoves, or
two young pigeons'. "

Lk 2:24

Commend yourself to St Joseph
ഇരു

*T*o other Saints Our Lord seems to have given power to succour us in some special necessity – but to this glorious Saint, I know by experience, He has given the power to help us in all. Our Lord would have us understand that as He was subject to St Joseph on earth – for St Joseph, bearing the title of father and being His guardian, could command Him – so now in Heaven Our Lord grants all his petitions. I have asked others to recommend themselves to St Joseph, and they, too, know the same thing by experience.

St Teresa of Avila, *Autobiography, VI, 9*

Prayer whereby St Joseph is chosen as patron
ഇരു

O Saint Joseph, faithful steward and guardian of Christ Jesus my Redeemer, most chaste spouse of the Virgin Mother of God, I (N.) choose you today as my singular patron and advocate, and firmly resolve that I shall never desert you, nor permit that anything should be done against your honour by anyone of those subject to me. From you therefore I humbly pray that you may deign to accept me as a perpetual servant, to instruct in doubtful matters, to console in adversities, and finally in the hour of death to defend and protect me.

Amen.

" *Behold, an angel of the Lord appeared to Joseph in*
dream and said: 'Rise, take the child and his mother an
flee to Egypt, and remain there till I tell you; for Hero
is about to search for the child, to destroy him.' "

Mt 2:1.

The Father of the Saviour
ഌരു

*W*ho deserved to be called and to be regarded as the father of our Saviour? We may draw a parallel between him and the great Patriarch. As the first Joseph was by the envy of his brothers sold and sent into Egypt, the second Joseph fled into Egypt with Christ to escape the envy of Herod. The chaste Patriarch remained faithful to his master, despite the evil suggestions of his mistress. St Joseph, recognizing in his wife the Virgin Mother of his Lord, guarded her with the utmost fidelity and chastity. To the Joseph of old was given interpretation of dreams, to the new Joseph a share in heavenly secrets.

St Bernard, *Homily 2, On the "Missus Est"*

Be with us in our Trials
ഌരു

*B*lessed Joseph, husband of Mary, be with us this day. You protected and cherished the Virgin; loving the Child Jesus as your Son, you rescued Him from the danger of death. Defend the Church, the household of God, purchased by the Blood of Christ.

Guardian of the Holy Family, be with us in our trials. May your prayers obtain for us the strength to flee from error and wrestle with the powers of corruption so that in life we may grow in holiness and in death rejoice in the crown of victory.

Amen.

" *I have made a covenant with my chosen one,*
I have sworn to David my servant:
'I will establish your descendants for ever,
and build your throne for all generations.' "

Ps 89:4-5

Saint Joseph Master of Prayer

ഇൻ

*E*specially persons of prayer should always be attached to him. For I don't know how one can think about the Queen of Angels and about when she went through so much with the Infant Jesus without giving thanks to St Joseph for the good assistance he then provided them both with. Those who cannot find a master to teach them prayer should take this glorious saint for their master, and they will not go astray.

St Teresa of Avila, *Autobiography, Ch. VI, 8*

Prayer to Saint Joseph for protection

ഇൻ

O Blessed St Joseph, who did accompany Jesus and Mary in all their journeys, and who has therefore merited to be called the patron of all travellers, accompany us in this journey through life. Be our guide and our protector; watch over us; preserve us from all accidents and dangers to soul and body; support us in our fatigue, and aid us to sanctify it by offering it to God. Make us ever mindful that we are strangers, sojourners here below; that heaven is our true home; and help us to persevere on the straight road that leads there. We beseech thee especially to protect and aid us in the last great voyage from time to eternity, so that, under thy guidance we may reach the realm of happiness and glory, there to repose eternally with thee in the company of Jesus and Mary.

Amen.

"*And he arose and took the young child and his mother by night He departed to Egypt and remained there until the death of Herod.*"

Mt 2:14-5

The power to assist us in all cases

𝕊𝕆𝕆ℝ

Some Saints are privileged to extend to us their patronage with particular efficacy in certain needs, but not in others; but our holy patron St Joseph has the power to assist us in all cases, in every necessity, in every undertaking.

St Thomas Aquinas, *IV. Sent. 9, 45*

We come to you, O blessed Joseph, in our distress. Having sought the aid of your most blessed spouse, we now confidently implore your assistance also.

We humbly beg that, mindful of the affection which bound you to the Immaculate Virgin Mother of God, and of the fatherly love with which you cherished the Child Jesus, you will lovingly watch over the heritage which Jesus Christ purchased with His blood, and by your powerful intercession help us in our urgent need.

Prudent guardian of the Holy Family, protect the chosen people of Jesus Christ; drive far from us, most loving father, all error and corrupting sin. From your place in heaven, most powerful protector, graciously come to our aid in this conflict with the powers of darkness, and, as of old you delivered the Child Jesus from danger of death, so now defend the holy Church from the snares of the enemy and from all adversity.

Extend to each one of us your continual protection, that, led on by your example, and borne up by your strength, we may be able to live and die in holiness and obtain everlasting happiness in heaven.

Amen.

Our Lord Jesus Christ as a child, that is, as one clothe[d]
in the fragility of human nature, had to grow and becom[e]
stronger but as the eternal Word of God, he had no need t[o]
become stronger or to grow. Hence he is rightly described [as]
full of wisdom and grace.

St Bede the Venerable, In Lucae Evangelium Exposit[io]

The Watchful Guardian of the Living Bread

෨ඏ

*L*et us consider this man Joseph in connection with the Universal Church of Christ. Is he not that elect and chosen one, through whom, and under whom, Christ is orderly and honestly brought into the world? If, then, the Holy Universal Church be under a debt to the Virgin Mother (because through her the Church has been made to receive Christ), next to Mary the Church owes thanks and reverence to Joseph. He verily is the key which unlocked the treasures of the Church of the Old Testament, for in his person all the excellence of Patriarchs and Prophets comes to the completion of achievement, seeing that he alone enjoyed in this life the full fruition of what God had been pleased to promise aforetime to them. It is therefore with good reason that we see a type of him in that Patriarch Joseph who stored up corn for the people. But the second Joseph has a more excellent dignity than the first, seeing that the first gave to the Egyptians bread only for the body, but the second was, on behalf of all the elect, the watchful guardian of that Living Bread which came down from heaven, of which whosoever eats will never die.

St Bernardine of Siena, *Sermon on St Joseph*

*G*od our Father, creator and ruler of the universe, in every age you call man to develop and use his gifts for the good of others. With St Joseph as our example and guide, help us to do the work you have asked and come to the rewards you have promised. We ask this through Jesus Christ, your Son, our Lord.

Amen.

"*She will bear a son, and you shall call his name Jesus, for he will save his people from their sins.*"

Mt 1:21

A shadow of the Heavenly Trinity

୧୦୧

*F*or thirty years Christ lived with Mary and Joseph, and thus formed a shadow of the Heavenly Trinity on earth. O the perfection of that sympathy which existed between the three! Not a look of one but the other two understood, as expressed, better than if expressed in a thousand words; nay, more than understood accepted, echoed, corroborated. It was like three instruments absolutely in tune, which all vibrate when one.

John Henry Newman, *Meditations and Devotions*

Prayer to ask for a special favour

୧୦୧

*G*lorious Saint Joseph, foster-father and protector of Jesus Christ, to you I raise my heart and my hands to implore your powerful intercession. Please obtain for me from the kind Heart of Jesus the help and the graces necessary for my spiritual and temporal welfare. I ask particularly for the grace of a happy death and the special favour I now implore. (Make your petition here ...)

Guardian of the Word Incarnate, I feel animated with confidence that your prayers on my behalf will be graciously heard before the throne of God. O glorious Saint Joseph, through the love you bear for Jesus Christ, and for the glory of His name, hear my prayers and obtain my petitions.

Amen.

"*But when Herod died, behold an angel of the Lord appeared in a dream to Joseph in Egypt, saying, 'Rise, take the child and his mother, and go to the land of Israel, for those who sought the child's life are dead.' And he rose and took the child and his mother, and went to the land of Israel.*"

Mt 2:19-21

Joseph, a just man
ଋୠ

*W*e venerate Joseph, a just man. Joseph, of the house of David, who loved Mary most deeply, because he accepted her whole mystery. We venerate Joseph in whom there is reflected more fully than in all earthly fathers the Fatherhood of God himself. We venerate Joseph who built the family house on earth for the Eternal Word just as Mary gave him a human body. "The Word became flesh and dwelt among us" (Jn 1:14).

From this great mystery of faith let us direct our thoughts to our homes, to so many couples and families. Joseph of Nazareth is a particular revelation of the dignity of human fatherhood! Joseph of Nazareth, the carpenter, the man of work. Think of that, you, precisely you men of work of ... the whole world.

The family rests on the dignity of human fatherhood – on the responsibility of the man, husband and father, as also on his work. Joseph of Nazareth bears witness to this for us.

Pope John Paul II, *19 March 1981*

*S*t Joseph, spouse of the Blessed Virgin Mary and foster father of the Son of God, in your authority, care and tenderness, you were a loving reflection of the Heavenly Father. You know the challenges with which all husbands and fathers are faced in the task of educating their children and providing for the needs of their families. Obtain for them the graces they need to raise their families according to the will of the Heavenly Father and to prepare them for eternity.

Amen.

He gave to Joseph a father's love,
a father's watchful care,
a father's authority.

Saint John Damascene

A community of gifts

෨ඦ

*A*s Joseph has been united to the Blessed Virgin by the ties of marriage, it may not be doubted that he approached nearer than any to the eminent dignity by which the Mother of God surpasses so nobly all created natures. For marriage is the most intimate of all unions which from its essence imparts a community of gifts between those that by it are joined together. Thus in giving Joseph the Blessed Virgin as spouse, God appointed him to be not only her life's companion, the witness of her maidenhood, the protector of her honour, but also, by virtue of the conjugal tie, a participator in her sublime dignity. And Joseph shines among all mankind by the most august dignity, since by divine will, he was the guardian of the Son of God and reputed as His father among men.

Pope Leo XIII, *Quamquam Pluries*

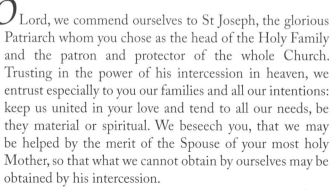

O Lord, we commend ourselves to St Joseph, the glorious Patriarch whom you chose as the head of the Holy Family and the patron and protector of the whole Church. Trusting in the power of his intercession in heaven, we entrust especially to you our families and all our intentions: keep us united in your love and tend to all our needs, be they material or spiritual. We beseech you, that we may be helped by the merit of the Spouse of your most holy Mother, so that what we cannot obtain by ourselves may be obtained by his intercession.

Amen.

"He shall cry to me, 'Thou art my Father, my God and the Rock of my salvation'."

Ps 89:26

*T*he example of Jesus Christ, who was pleased when on earth so to honour and to be obedient to St Joseph, should alone be sufficient to inflame us all to be very devout to this great Saint. Suarez says that St Joseph, next to Mary, surpasses all the other saints in merit and glory. We should particularly entertain devotion to St Joseph, that he may obtain for us a happy death. In return for having delivered the Infant Jesus from the snares of Herod, he has the privilege of delivering the dying from the snares of the devil.

St Alphonsus

Prayer of Pope John XXIII for Fathers
ഇരു

*S*aint Joseph, guardian of Jesus and chaste husband of Mary, you passed your life in loving fulfilment of duty. You supported the holy family of Nazareth with the work of your hands. Kindly protect those who trustingly come to you. You know their aspirations, their hardships, their hopes. They look to you because they know you will understand and protect them. You too knew trial, labour and weariness. But amid the worries of material life, your soul was full of deep peace and sang out in true joy through intimacy with God's Son entrusted to you and with Mary, his tender Mother. Assure those you protect that they do not labour alone. Teach them to find Jesus near them and to watch over Him faithfully as you have done.

Amen.

"*Whatever your task, work heartily, as serving the Lord and not men, knowing that from the Lord you will receive the inheritance as your reward; you are serving the Lord Christ.*"

Col 3:23-24

*T*he mystery of the Incarnation consecrates the thirty years of life spent in the silence of Nazareth with Mary and Joseph… From the hidden life rises the canticle in praise of the dignity and greatness of the family, in praise of the sacred duty of labour and its nobility.

Pope John XXIII, *4 Oct 1962*

Prayer to St Joseph, as Patron of Workers
(John XXIII)

*B*lessed St Joseph, patron of all working people, obtain for me the grace to labour in a spirit of penance for the atonement of my many sins. Help me to be conscientious in my work so that I may give as full a measure as I have received.

May I labour in a spirit of thankfulness and joy, ever mindful of all the gifts I have received from God that enable me to perform these tasks. Permit me to work in peace, patience, and moderation, keeping in mind the account I must one day give of time lost, talents unused, good omitted, and vanity of success, so fatal to the work of God. Glorious St Joseph, may my labours be all for Jesus, all through Mary, and all after your holy example in life and in death.

Amen.

"Whoever honours his father atones for sins, and whoever glorifies his mother is like one who lays up treasure."

Sir 3:3-4

Saint Joseph, faithful and wise servant

*I*he first Joseph laid bread by, not for himself only, but for all the people. The second Joseph received into his keeping the Living Bread which came down from heaven, and he kept the same, not for himself only, but for all the world. Without doubt, good and faithful was this Joseph who espoused the Mother of the Saviour. Indeed, he is that faithful and wise servant whom the Lord hath made ruler over his Household. For the Lord appointed him to be the comfort of his Mother, the keeper of his own body, and, in a word, the chief and most trusty helper on earth in carrying out the eternal counsels.

St Bernard, *Homily 2, On the "Missus Est"*

Prayer for assistance with a difficult problem

O glorious St Joseph, you who have power to render possible even things which are considered impossible, come to our aid in our present trouble and distress. Take this important and difficult affair under your particular protection, that it may end happily. (Name your request.)

O dear St Joseph, all our confidence is in you. Let it not be said that we would invoke you in vain; and since you are so powerful with Jesus and Mary, show that your goodness equals your power.

Amen.

" And when they had performed everything according
the law of the Lord, they returned into Galilee, to the
own city, Nazareth. "

Lk 2:

There is a close connection between work and the fami
between your work and your family. St Joseph is, with
special right, the Patron Saint of this bond.

Pope John Paul II, 19 March 19

Saint Joseph, the Craftsman

৪০৫৪

*A*t the same time, the Church venerates Joseph of Nazareth as a "craftsman", as a man of work, perhaps a carpenter by trade. He was the one and only – among all the men of work on earth – at whose workbench there appeared every day Jesus Christ, Son of God and Son of man. It was Joseph himself who had him learn the work of his profession, who started him on his way in it, who taught him to overcome the difficulties and the resistance of the "material" element and to draw out of shapeless matter the works of human handicraft. It is he, Joseph of Nazareth, who once for all linked the Son of God to human work. Thanks to him, the same Christ belongs also to the world of work and gives witness to its very high dignity in the eyes of God.

Pope John Paul II, *19 March 1982*

Prayer to Saint Joseph, the Workman

৪০৫৪

*W*e speak to you, O blessed Joseph, our protector on earth, as one who knows the value of work and the response of our calling. We address you through your holy spouse, the Immaculate Virgin Mother of God, and knowing the fatherly affection with which you embraced Our Lord Jesus, ask that you may assist us in our needs, and strengthen us in our labours.

Be our watchful guardian in our work, our defender and strength against injustice and errors. As we look to your example and seek your assistance, support us in our every effort, that we may come to everlasting rest with you in the blessedness of heaven.

Amen.

"*The child grew and became strong, filled with wisdom; and the favour of God was upon him.*"

Lk 2:40

Ordinary Life

Good St Joseph! Oh! How I love him! … I can see him planing, then drying his forehead from time to time. Oh! How I pity him! It seems to me their life was simple. … What does me a lot of good when I think of the Holy Family is to imagine a life that was very ordinary. It wasn't everything that they have told us or imagined. For example, that the Child Jesus, after having formed some birds out of clay, breathed upon them and gave them life. Ah! no! little Jesus didn't perform useless miracles like that, even to please His Mother. Why weren't they transported into Egypt by a miracle which would have been necessary and so easy for God. In the twinkling of an eye, they could have been brought there. No, everything in their life was done just as in our own.

How many troubles, disappointments! How many times did others make complaints to good St Joseph! How many times did they refuse to pay him for his work! Oh! How astonished we would be if we only knew how much they had to suffer!

St Thérèse of Lisieux, *Last Conversations, 20 August 1897*

O God, Creator of all things, you have given the law of work for the human race. Your Son Jesus Christ himself embraced this law and, willingly labouring under the guidance of St Joseph, he sanctified work. Mercifully grant that, following the same example and patronage of St Joseph, we may fulfil the works which you command and obtain the rewards which you promise.

Amen.

"Behold, your father and I have been looking for you anxiously."

Lk 2:48-50

The Finding in the Temple

ೞೞ

Christ's mother and foster-father seek for their son in the greatest distress. At last they find him, and rebuke him, as St Luke tells us so vividly, and they take him back to Nazareth with them. And that is just what happens to holy men who have been given souls to look after, or who have been charged to preach the word of God. And I think that for them the Holy Spirit is foster-father, while their mother is none other than Charity herself. Together they shower blessings and kindness on us who have souls in our care, encouraging us to journey on towards God, feeding and nourishing us with the twofold milk of love of God and of neighbour. Together they keep and sustain and refresh us as we strive for the things of God, just as Mary and Joseph supported the boy Jesus during the years of his youth at Nazareth.

St Aelred of Rievaulx, *On Jesus at Twelve Years Old*

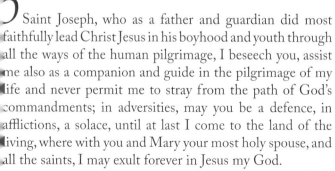

O Saint Joseph, who as a father and guardian did most faithfully lead Christ Jesus in his boyhood and youth through all the ways of the human pilgrimage, I beseech you, assist me also as a companion and guide in the pilgrimage of my life and never permit me to stray from the path of God's commandments; in adversities, may you be a defence, in afflictions, a solace, until at last I come to the land of the living, where with you and Mary your most holy spouse, and all the saints, I may exult forever in Jesus my God.

Amen.

And he said to them, 'How is it that you sought me? Did you not know that I must be in my Father's house?' And they did not understand the saying which he spoke to them.

Lk 2:49-50

*M*arvellous is thy sublime elevation, O Joseph! O incomparable dignity, that the Mother of God, the Queen of Heaven, the Sovereign Lady of the world, should not disdain to call thee her lord! Truly, truly, I know not which most to admire, the great humility of Mary, or the sublime grandeur of Joseph.

Jean Gerson

Consecration to Saint Joseph
(of Children by their Parents)

O glorious St Joseph, to you God committed the care of His only begotten Son amid the many dangers of this world. We come to you and ask you to take under your special protection the children God has given us. Through holy baptism they became children of God and members of His holy Church. We consecrate them to you today, that through this consecration they may become your foster children. Guard them, guide their steps in life, form their hearts after the hearts of Jesus and Mary.

St Joseph, who felt the tribulation and worry of a parent when the child Jesus was lost, protect our dear children for time and eternity. May you be their father and counsellor. Let them, like Jesus, grow in age as well as in wisdom and grace before God and men. Preserve them from the corruption of this world, and give us the grace one day to be united with them in heaven forever.

Amen.

By the name of father, no angel, no saint merited to be called; Joseph alone could so be called.

St Basil

The Seven Sorrows and Joys of St Joseph
෧෮

Say seven Our Fathers and seven Hail Marys and seven Glory Bes in honour of the seven sorrows and seven joys of St Joseph while calling them to mind.

The Annunciation to St Joseph: sorrow: the doubt of St Joseph; joy: the revelation of the mystery of the Incarnation.

The Birth of Our Lord: sorrow: at not finding a suitable place for the Child and His Mother; joy: the birth of the Saviour of the world.

The Circumcision: sorrow: the sight of the Precious Blood; joy: in naming the Child *Jesus*.

The Prophecy of Simeon in the Temple: sorrow: at the suffering foretold of Jesus and Mary; joy: the redemption of the world.

The Flight into Egypt: sorrow: the danger to the Child's life; joy: at bringing the Child safely to Egypt, being with Him.

The Return to Israel: sorrow: the danger of Herod to the Child; joy: in bringing the Child and His Mother out of Egypt and settling in Nazareth.

The Child is lost and found in the Temple: sorrow: separation from the lost Child and concern for Him; joy: finding the Child and returning with Him to Nazareth.

SANCTE JOSEPH

Joseph is a paradise of delights.

St Ephrem

*I*f Mary was the aurora preceding the Divine Sun, Joseph was the horizon illuminated by its splendours.

St Leonard of Port Maurice

Prayer to St Joseph
(by Pope Leo XIII)

ৎ০০৪

*T*o you, O blessed Joseph, do we come in our tribulation, and having implored the help of your most holy spouse, we confidently invoke your patronage also. Through that charity which bound you to the immaculate Virgin Mother of God and through the paternal love with which you embraced the Child Jesus, we humbly beg you graciously to regard the inheritance which Jesus Christ has purchased by his Blood, and with your power and strength to aid us in our necessities.

O most watchful Guardian of the Holy Family, defend the chosen children of Jesus Christ; O most loving Father, ward off from us every contagion of error and corrupting influence; O our most mighty protector, be propitious to us and from heaven assist us in our struggle with the power of darkness; and, as once you rescued the Child Jesus from deadly peril, so now protect God's Holy Church from the snares of the enemy and from all adversity; shield, too, each one of us by your constant protection, so that, supported by your example and your aid, we may be able to live piously, to die holily, and to obtain eternal happiness in heaven.

Amen.

Praises of Saint Joseph
(composed by St John Eudes)

೫೦೪

*H*ail, Joseph, image of God the Father,
Hail, Joseph, father of God the Son,
Hail, Joseph, temple of the Holy Spirit,
Hail, Joseph, beloved of the Most Holy Trinity,
Hail, Joseph, most faithful coadjutor of the great counsel,
Hail, Joseph, most worthy Spouse of the Virgin Mary,
Hail, Joseph, father of all the faithful,
Hail, Joseph, guardian of all those who have embraced
  virginity,

Hail, Joseph, faithful observer of holy silence,

Hail, Joseph, lover of holy poverty,

Hail, Joseph, model of meekness and patience,

Hail, Joseph, mirror of humility and obedience;

Blessed art thou above all men,

Blessed thine eyes, which have seen the things which thou hast seen,

Blessed thine ears, which have heard the things which thou hast heard,

Blessed thy hands, which have touched and handled the Incarnate Word,

Blessed thine arms, which have borne Him who bears all things,

Blessed thy bosom, on which the Son of God fondly rested,

Blessed thy heart, inflamed with burning love,

Blessed be the Eternal Father, Who chose thee,

Blessed be the Son, Who loved thee,

Blessed be the Holy Spirit, Who sanctified thee,

Blessed be Mary, thy Spouse, who cherished thee as her Spouse and brother,

Blessed be the Angel who served thee as a guardian,

And blessed forever be all who love and bless thee.

Amen.

" *The souls of the righteous are in the hand of God, and no torment will ever touch them.* "

Wis 3:1

ovena of Prayer through the Intercession of Saint Joseph

*G*od our Father,

u welcome near You those who serve You faithfully in
.s world: we invoke Saint Joseph because of his love for
u and his closeness to your Son Jesus. His fatherly care
· Jesus was a sign of your provident and caring fatherhood
wards all. I beg You to grant the prayer I make to You in
th as I entrust myself to his intercession.

Our Father

*L*ord Jesus,

ly Son of God and our Saviour, remember that St Joseph
ent his life here below in your service and the service of
ur Immaculate mother Mary. Because he was her beloved
ouse and was completely dedicated to your well-being, we
ay to him. I depend on You to grant the graces I implore
rough his intercession.

Hail Mary

*H*oly Spirit,

urce of all grace and all love, it is through your action that
nt Joseph was so filled with attention for the divine plan
d responded to God's will with such perfect fidelity.
ace he intercedes for us and for the whole Church now, we
y through him. I ask You to inspire and to hear my prayer,
that there may be granted to me the favour entrusted to
intercession.

Glory be to the Father

Three days of Prayer to Saint Joseph

(by John Henry Newman)

℀℣

First Day

CONSIDER THE GLORIOUS TITLES OF ST JOSEPH:

HE was the true and worthy Spouse of Mary, supplying in a visible manner the place of Mary's Invisible Spouse the Holy Ghost. He was a virgin, and his virginity was the faithful mirror of the virginity of Mary. He was the Cherub, placed to guard the new terrestrial Paradise from the intrusion of every foe.

℣. Blessed be the name of Joseph.
℟. Henceforth and forever. Amen.

Let us pray

God, who in Thine ineffable Providence didst vouchsaf to choose Blessed Joseph to be the husband of Thy most holy Mother, grant, we beseech Thee, that we may be made worthy to receive him for our intercessor in heaven whom on earth we venerate as our holy Protector: who livest and reignest world without end. Amen.

Consider the Glorious Titles of St Joseph:

HIS was the title of father of the Son of God, because he was the Spouse of Mary, ever Virgin. He was our Lord's father, because Jesus ever yielded to him the obedience of a son. He was our Lord's father, because to him were entrusted, and by him were faithfully fulfilled, the duties of a father, in protecting Him, giving Him a home, sustaining and rearing Him, and providing Him with a trade.

Blessed be the name of Joseph.
Henceforth and for ever. Amen.

Let us pray
God, who in Thine ineffable Providence didst vouchsafe, &c.

Consider the Glorious Titles of St Joseph:

HE is Holy Joseph, because according to the opinion of a great number of doctors, he, as well as St John Baptist, was sanctified even before he was born. He is Holy Joseph, because his office, of being spouse and protector of Mary, specially demanded sanctity. He is Holy Joseph, because no other Saint but he lived in such and so long intimacy and familiarity with the source of all holiness, Jesus, God incarnate, and Mary, the holiest of creatures.

Blessed be the name of Joseph.
Henceforth and for ever. Amen.

Let us pray
God, who in Thine ineffable Providence didst vouchsafe, &c.

*O what a moment of sympathy between the three, †
moment before Joseph died – they supporting and hang†
over him, he looking at them and reposing in them w‗
undivided, unreserved, supreme, devotion, for he was
the arms of God and the Mother of God. As a flame sho‗
up and expires, so was the ecstasy of that last mome‗
ineffable, for each knew and thought of the reverse wh‗
was to follow on the snapping of that bond.*

John Henry Newman, Meditations and Devoti‗

St Joseph, Patron of a Happy Death

৩০৪৩

Since we all must die, we should cherish a special devotion to St Joseph, that he may obtain for us a happy death. All Christians regard him as the advocate of the dying who assists at the hour of death those who honoured him during their life, and they do so for three reasons:

First, because Jesus Christ loved him not only as a friend, but as a father, and on this account his mediation is far more efficacious than that of any other Saint.

Second, because St Joseph has obtained special power against the evil spirits, who tempt us with redoubled vigour at the hour of death.

Third, the assistance given St Joseph at his death by Jesus and Mary obtained for him the right to secure a holy and peaceful death for his servants. Hence, if they invoke him at the hour of death he will not only help them, but he will also obtain for them the assistance of Jesus and Mary.

St Alphonsus

O Glorious St Joseph, behold I choose thee today for my special patron in life and at the hour of my death. Preserve and increase in me the spirit of prayer and fervour in the service of God. Remove far from me every kind of sin; obtain for me that my death may not come upon me unawares, but that I may have time to confess my sins sacramentally and to bewail them with a most perfect understanding and a most sincere and perfect contrition, in order that I may breathe forth my soul into the hands of Jesus and Mary.

Amen.

" *Who then is the faithful and wise servant, whom his master has set over his household, to give them their food at the proper time? Blessed is that servant whom his master when he comes will find so doing. Truly I say to you, he will set him over his possessions.* "

Mt 24:45-47

St Joseph accomplished the mission of being the guardian and provider for Mary and Jesus most faithfully, and for this reason the Lord addressed him with those words: 'Well done, good and faithful servant, enter thou into the joy of thy Lord.'

St Bernardine of Siena

Prayer to St Joseph for the Whole Church
ஸௐ

O Glorious Saint Joseph, you were chosen by God to be the foster father of Jesus, the most pure spouse of Mary, ever Virgin, and the head of the Holy Family. You have been chosen by Christ's Vicar as the heavenly Patron and Protector of the Church founded by Christ.

Protect the Sovereign Pontiff and all bishops and priests united with him. Be the protector of all who labour for souls amid the trials and tribulations of this life; and grant that all peoples of the world may be docile to the Church without which there is no salvation.

Dear Saint Joseph, accept the offering I make to you. Be my father, protector, and guide in the way of salvation. Obtain for me purity of heart and a love for the spiritual life. After your example, let all my actions be directed to the greater glory of God, in union with the Divine Heart of Jesus, the Immaculate Heart of Mary, and your own paternal heart. Finally, pray for me that I may share in the peace and joy of your holy death.

Amen.

Litany of Saint Joseph

ഇൻൽ

Lord, have mercy. Lord, have mercy.

Christ, have mercy. Christ, have mercy.

Lord, have mercy. Lord, have mercy.

Christ, hear us. Christ, graciously hear us.

God, the Father of Heaven, have mercy on us.

God the Son, Redeemer of the world, have mercy on us.

God the Holy Spirit, have mercy on us.

Holy Trinity, One God, have mercy on us.

Holy Mary, pray for us.

St Joseph, pray for us.

Renowned offspring of David, pray for us.

Light of Patriarchs, pray for us.

Spouse of the Mother of God, pray for us.

Chaste guardian of the Virgin, pray for us.

Foster father of the Son of God, pray for us.

Diligent protector of Christ, pray for us.

Head of the Holy Family, pray for us.

Joseph most just, pray for us.

Joseph most chaste, pray for us.

Joseph most prudent, pray for us.

Joseph most strong, pray for us.

Joseph most obedient, pray for us.

Joseph most faithful, pray for us.

Mirror of patience, pray for us.

over of poverty, pray for us.
odel of artisans, pray for us.
ory of home life, pray for us.
uardian of virgins, pray for us.
llar of families, pray for us.
lace of the wretched, pray for us.
ope of the sick, pray for us.
tron of the dying, pray for us.
rror of demons, pray for us.
otector of Holy Church, pray for us.

mb of God, who takes away the sins of the world,
are us, O Lord!

mb of God, who takes away the sins of the world,
aciously hear us, O Lord!

mb of God, who takes away the sins of the world,
ve mercy on us.

He made him the lord of his household.
And prince over all his possessions.

t us pray.

O God, in your ineffable providence you were pleased to
hoose Blessed Joseph to be the spouse of your most holy
Mother; grant, we beg you, that we may be worthy to have
im for our intercessor in heaven whom on earth we venerate
s our Protector: You who live and reign forever and ever.

Amen.

Acknowledgements
෨෨෬

Cover picture: courtesy of Etablissement Saint Joseph, Carpentras; p. 1: Saint Josecharpentier, George de la Tour, Besançon, Musée des Beaux-Arts et d'Archéolo
© RMN / droits réservés; p. 4: Icône de la Sainte Famille, Art: Sr Marie Paul OSI
Monastère des Bénédictines du Mont des Oliviers and Editions CHOISIR, Genè
p. 6: L'Apparition de l'ange à saint Joseph, dit aussi le Songe de saint Jose
Georges de la Tour, Nantes, Musée des Beaux-Arts © Photo RMN / Gérard Blo
8: The Wedding of Mary and Joseph, St Mary the Virgin parish church, Freela
Oxfordshire © Photograph Lawrence Lew OP; p. 10: St Dominic's Priory chu
London © Photograph Lawrence Lew OP; p. 12: La Nativité, Philippe de Champaig
Lille, Palais des Beaux-Arts © RMN / Philippe Bernard; p. 14: Peterhouse Coll
chapel, Cambridge © Photograph Lawrence Lew OP; p. 16: Psautier d'Ingeburge
Danemark, reine de France, Présentation au Temple, Chantilly, Musée Condé, M
Fo 16 verso © RMN (Domaine de Chantilly) / René-Gabriel Ojéda; p. 18: St Jos
aux colombes, Art: Sr Marie Paul OSB © Monastère des Bénédictines du Mont
Oliviers and Editions CHOISIR, Genève; p. 20: The Return from Egypt, St Mary
Virgin parish church, Freeland, Oxfordshire © Photograph Lawrence Lew OP; p.
St Joseph, Ninian Comper, Downside Abbey © Photograph Lawrence Lew OP; p.
The Flight to Egypt, Our Lady of Victories church, South Kensington © Photogr
Lawrence Lew OP; p. 26: Exeter College chapel, Oxford © Photograph Lawrence I
OP; p. 28: The Holy Family, Westminster Cathedral © Photograph Lawrence Lew
p. 30: Bibliothèque municipale de Tours, Ms 2283, Fo 21 (Fuite en Egy
© CNRS-IRHT; p. 32: Holy Family icon, David Clayton; p. 34: St Joseph, Nia
Comper, Southwark Cathedral © Photograph Lawrence Lew OP; p. 36: St Jos
and the Child Jesus, Eric Gill, courtesy of St Joseph's Parish church, Picker
p. 38: Sagrada Familia, Juan del Castillo © Museo de Bellas Artes de Sevill
40: Notre Dame de France, Leicester Square © Photograph Lawrence Lew O
42: Jesus discovered in the Temple, Simone Martini, Walker Gallery, Liverpoc
National Museums Liverpool; p. 44: St Alban's Cathedral © Photograph Lawre
Lew OP; p. 46: Rosary Basilica, Lourdes © Photograph Lawrence Lew OP; p.
Carmelite church, Salamanca © Photograph Lawrence Lew OP; p. 50: Icône
St Joseph, Art: Sr Marie Paul OSB © Monastère des Bénédictines du Mont
Oliviers and Editions CHOISIR, Genève; p. 52: Psautier d'Ingeburge de Danem
reine de France, La Fuite en Egypte, Chantilly, Musée Condé, Ms 9 Fo 18 v
© RMN (Domaine de Chantilly) / René-Gabriel Ojéda; p. 54: La Muerte de San J
Juan del Castillo © Museo de Bellas Artes de Sevilla; p. 56: Nativity, reprodu
by permission of the Vicar and Churchwardens of All Saints, Margaret Stree
Photograph Lawrence Lew OP; p. 58: Altar carving, courtesy of the Fathers of
Oxford Oratory; p. 60: Cristo coronando a San José, Francisco de Zurbarán © M
de Bellas Artes de Sevilla; p. 63: La fuite en Egypte © Bibliothèque municipal
Lyon, Ms 244, Fo 178.